3-06

Cartwheel to the Moon

Cartwheel to the Moon
My Sicilian Childhood
Poems by Emanuel di Pasquale

Selected and Arranged by Marianne Carus
Introduction by X. J. Kennedy
Illustrated by K. Dyble Thompson

Cricket Books
Chicago

For Elisabeth with love. —E. di P.

To my brother John: Chi ama il suo lavoro lo
fa bene. —K. D. T.

Some poems in this collection first appeared in other
publications. See page 64 for acknowledgments.

Text copyright © 2003 by Emanuel di Pasquale
Illustrations copyright © 2003 by K. Dyble Thompson
All rights reserved
Printed in the United States of America
Designed by Ron McCutchan
First edition, 2003

Library of Congress Cataloging-in-Publication Data

Di Pasquale, Emanuel, 1943–
    Cartwheel to the moon: my Sicilian childhood: poems / by
Emanuel di Pasquale; selected and arranged by Marianne Carus;
introduction by X. J. Kennedy; illustrated by K. Dyble Thompson.
— 1st ed.
    p. cm.
Summary: An illustrated collection of poems celebrating the land-
scape, people, plants and animals, customs and traditions of the
Italian island of Sicily.
    ISBN 0-8126-2679-6 (cloth : alk. paper)
    1. Sicily (Italy)—Juvenile poetry. 2. Children's poetry,
American.
    [1. Sicily (Italy)—Poetry. 2. Italy—Poetry. 3. American poetry.] I.
Carus, Marianne. II. Thompson, Kathryn Dyble, ill. III. Title.
    PS3554.I625 C37 2003
    811'.54--dc21

                                              2002152826

INTRODUCTION

$\mathcal{G}$etting up at dawn to see a hawk circle the sky. Swimming in the sea, going home with sand between your toes. Catching a baby crab that races over your hands. Biting into a cloud of cotton candy that gives you a sticky beard. Dressing in your best clothes to go to church— not to pray, this time, but to watch fireworks. Buying birds from a pet shop and letting them fly away. Marveling at stone tools left by a people who vanished thousands of years ago.

Those are only a few of the small adventures you'll share when you read these poems. You'll glimpse what it was like to grow up in colorful Sicily, in the Mediterranean Sea. Look at a map of Europe and you'll soon find Italy, shaped like a boot, and near its toe, the island of Sicily. As these poems reveal, Sicily is a land of almond trees and fig trees, of very old villages with fountains and tall churches, of looming mountains and—never far off—the blue, surrounding sea.

Sicilians are islanders, a fact that sets them apart from people who live on the mainland of Italy. They have their own language and customs. Like the poet himself, they have quick, warm feelings. They love music and dancing and celebrations—as you'll see from these poems.

Emanuel di Pasquale was born in Ragusa, in southern Sicily, on January 25, 1943. At that time, World War II was raging. Then, and for years after, life for most Sicilians was very hard. When Emanuel was only a baby, his father died. As a boy of eleven he had to drop out of school and work in a bakery to help feed his family. When he was thirteen years old, his mother, hoping for a better life, brought him to America. At that time, Emanuel knew little English, but at Sleepy Hollow High School in

North Tarrytown, New York, he quickly learned. Now, in a New Jersey college, he teaches students born in America how to use and understand their own language. He is, I've heard, a wonderful teacher. No doubt his younger daughter, Elisabeth, whom he loves to read books with, would agree.

Whether writing for kids or for grownups, Emanuel di Pasquale writes straight from his heart. He makes you feel what he feels. Some of his works have won prizes. One of his best rewards came lately, when, returning for a visit to his hometown of Ragusa, he was interviewed on TV and given a warm welcome.

Reading Emanuel di Pasquale's poems, I can practically see, hear, smell, touch, and taste Sicily. These are poems that seem to reach out and grasp real things. Di Pasquale weaves words into music that stays with you. I can't forget an amazing short poem called "Rain," from his book *Genesis*. Here it is, all of it: "Like a drummer's brush / the rain hushes the surface of tin porches." Just read that little poem out loud to yourself. Try to remember it and say it again. Hear those S sounds? You can almost imagine you're out in the rain yourself, hearing it beat down with a steady *sh-h-h-h-h*.

Cartwheel to the Moon may be a slim book, but it has taken years and years to grow. Although magazines (especially *Cricket*) and many children's anthologies have been printing Emanuel di Pasquale's poems for a long time, we haven't ever before had a whole book of them. Read them and take your time, and above all, just enjoy them. Imagine you're a kid like young Emanuel. Maybe a door will swing open for you upon another land, a Sicily both real and magical.

—X. J. Kennedy

Cartwheel to the Moon

PROLOGUE
Sicilian Villages

*L*ook at the hilly Sicilian villages:
walls of stone houses chewed up by moon tides,
sun swells,
their blue or yellow faces cracked,
left cracked.
Look at the steep hill roads,
each rectangular stone pinched by a hand pick
to help the old on their way to Matins
find traction in the frosty dawns.
And see the public fountain, pouring.
Stop and drink from cupped hands.

Look at the low clay roofs and the nesting swallows.
Finally, climb the cathedral towers and see farms
and orchards girdling the villages,
and reach out into the valleys
where small rivers
meander
and where young boys swim naked,
their clothes strewn
among bamboo thickets.

Spring

"Things Grow in Laughter."

The sun has a tail
that reaches under the earth
and tickles seeds.
That's what grandmother
once told me.
She says things grow
in laughter.

Mid-March bareness is rough
on hide-and-seek.
A few hardheaded leaves hang on
and like brass trinkets
crick crack the wind.
An owl hums . . . whho . . . whho . . .
Phone lines are shiny snakes.
The hills are red-headed boys
with tough crew cuts.

Wingtips dancing,
stretching its shadow ahead of itself,
the hawk startles the sun.
Treetops reach out to it,
and the leftover moon leans down.

17

This April night,
the moon is like a loose sunflower;
it rests on the shoulders of the trees,
leaps over the woods,
and rides on a sea of lights.

$\mathcal{I}$n the early morning,
when Grandmother wakes
at my house,
she looks at the small
yellow flowers that
leak all over the yard
and thinks she's in heaven.

It's windy and my mother
tries to close the window shut.
But I won't let her.
I want to hear the sparrows sing,
and I want to let
the cool light of the moon touch me.

I like to watch
my mother dance.
The wind is her partner,
pulling her this way
and that way,
tiring her out,
making her laugh.

My neighbor always buys a lamb
for Easter butchering,
and ties it by his door,
and feeds it sweetest grass.
In the early mornings,
before I run down the river
to swim naked
and to let tadpoles slide
through my toes,
I plunge my hands into its deep wool.
Then, before Easter Sunday,
the lamb is seen no more.
And I think of the Easter Rebirth,
when Christ heals His wounds,
and I jump from the highest stairs
and roll His name
on the tip of my tight tongue
and fall and fall
and never get hurt,
while swallows circle
like black halos
over my head.

Summer

"I'll Cartwheel to the Moon."

I do cartwheels.
One day I'll cartwheel to a mountain,
and from the mountain
I'll cartwheel to the moon.

Mother and I
rip two rosebuds
from the rosebush in our yard,
and we slip a bit of branch
into each rosebud
and make ourselves pipes.
Then we puff on them
and laugh and laugh.

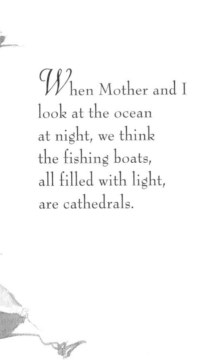

I like the feel of sand
between my toes.
It tickles.
Mother washes her feet
and insists that I wash mine.
But I won't.
I like to take a bit
of the ocean home.

*W*hen Mother and I
look at the ocean
at night, we think
the fishing boats,
all filled with light,
are cathedrals.

My Father

Once, while eating bread, I bit my lip
and spilled a little blood:
My father touched my face, gently,
and told me, "Little one, go on and eat
your bread; the bleeding will stop soon."
I mumbled something about tasting blood.
And he smiled and said, "It's your own blood."
That's the first thing I remember about him.

Then he walked on to the fair,
and I rode the carousel many times
on a large, yellow horse.
He paid double and stood next to me
and held me all the while.
I remember all the colors—red, blue, pink.

In all that light, I couldn't see the sky.
And the many sounds—like bells and small pianos;
my father bought cotton candy;
he thought it stuck to my face like a
scraggly, white beard.

I remember falling asleep over his large shoulder;
when he walked, he walked close to the houses,
and his shoulders were bent forward
and he was so tall, so strong, I thought.

My father had a mustache that tickled
even my mother; I don't remember this
because he had gone away by then, but she
used to tell me how he would come from work,
sneak up to her and tickle her face;
how they both would laugh.

I remember water, jumping in a pool of river
water in his arms—and I remember water bugs
swimming like bits of branches;
I helped him roast small crabs that we found
under small rocks; they tasted warm and sweet—
and we ate watermelon that he had placed
in the river to cool.

On the way home from the river, we stopped
and watched horses drink from the water trough;
the horses drank and were serious—
they blinked their eyes and snorted.
Then he took me to a cave—it was so cool inside,
and we drank from a mountain spring
that trickled down. I slurped the water
making believe I was a horse.
My father cupped his hands and filled them
with water and drank.
I asked him to let me drink from his cupped hands,
and he let me.

My father worked at a mine where they
would make cement; they would break
large rocks and shatter them
into cement powder; it was all to help build houses,
my mother said. I didn't know he even worked then.
My mother began telling me stories of my father
after he left—died, she said.
He didn't leave. He stood still,
my mother said. We would visit him where he slept,
unseen, in silence. There was earth
and a white rock and a picture of him
with his large mustache on the rock.
I would speak to him, but he would
(couldn't, my mother said) never answer.
We'd always bring flowers.

Every night he'd bring some flowers home.
He'd pick them from the meadows on his way home
from work, my mother told me.
Daisies, lilacs, marjoram.
And so we'd fill his grave with meadow flowers;

in November, on the Day of the Dead,
we'd bring white and yellow chrysanthemums.

My mother would tell me stories.
She'd say, "Your father would get up in the night,
for he had a long way to walk to work;
he loved us and he told me how he especially
loved your smile and your shining eyes."

I learned even more about his strength from her.
She said, "People loved him and he was blessed;
he knew how to care for animals—farmers
would call him when their horses
or sheep got ill,
and he knew how to help them into health.
I remember him always coming home
with bags of fruit, slabs of cheese,
and chickens the farmers gave him
as thanks for his help. He loved
to fill the house with fruits.

"In the summer, we would go to the sea.
He'd hire horse and cart and though
it took us five hours to get there, he liked
it that way. He never liked cars.
We would stop on the way to pick mulberries,
figs, prickly pears. The farmers knew him
and wouldn't charge him a thing.
He held you on his chest
and sat on the tip of the tongue of the sea;
first, he would drink a mouthful of seawater;
it made him thirsty for a little wine
which he liked to drink later on at lunch."

Some of my older friends remember my father—
I heard one evening he came home late,
and some of the children who always waited for him
(for he'd try to bring candies or shiny pebbles
for the little ones) ran up to him—
how he stood in the middle of the small street
and emptied his pockets of almonds
he had picked from trees on his way home,
and how after having emptied his pockets
he lifted his shirt
from his belt and a mountain of almonds
fell from his chest—
and the children scattered like wild birds
to grab the cascading almonds.

Lastly, I remember a stillness in the house—
it must have been when he forgot to live,
a silence—so many people and so few sounds
and later too many flowers
in our little house
and a smell too sweet, too heavy,
like darkness in moonless night.

Fall

"The Sea Gulls Fly Standing Still."

$\mathcal{I}$ pull a baby crab
off a seaweed-rich rock
and let it run on my hands,
and I see God. I see God
in millions of lights
dancing in the sea and air.
Hear Him in the wail of a street vendor
selling parsley and basil.
Hear Him in my own squeals
as I'm outrun by a foaming wave.
Feel Him in the smooth circling
of swallows,
in the quick beat of pigeons
landing in the cracks of clay roofs.
And I see God in the jasmine flower:
white and spread out as a gown
that dawn winds lift.

The statue of Saint John
is carried by thirty men
all around town—
I know some of the men;
they are my uncles and cousins.
My mother sweeps
in front of the house;
I help her.
She wants the street clean
when the saint blesses us.
The old women pray
as the statue goes by—
people pin money on it;
the priests sing and
look serious.

At night, we walk up to the church
to watch the fireworks.
We dress in our best clothes,
buy dry chickpeas, candies.
I hold my father's hand.
We watch the screaming,
spinning wheels—
the fireworks begin
and the church walls
seem to catch fire—
red, pink, and blue
colors burst all over.
Flowers of light
burn in the sky.
I never fall asleep
until all the fires are out.
Then we go home.

The wind from the northeast
is wild.
        The waves are wild.
The sea gulls fly standing still.

Intermittent
streams,
        the leaves
flow
in the current
of the fall winds
that handpick
the crackling
colors
        and make
oceans of the skies.

After a long silence,
a few birds sing.
They're back, swallows and
sparrows,
singing along with hardheaded leaves
that hang on high branches
and crick crack the wind,
singing as my sister and I,
half-drowned in red and
yellow fallen leaves,
join them with our shouts.

$\mathcal{B}$elow the hill, the cemetery sits,
a small city of the perfectly behaved.
Among the bushes and grass and pine trees
statues of angels rest their wings.
Like a goat, I hop on tombstones
and stone walls. My mother calls,
"Come down, you might get hurt."
I run to where two lions
guard the cemetery's gate.
One sleeps and one's wide-eyed.
I turn away from the sleeping lion.
Always, always I ride the wide-eyed beast.

$\mathcal{L}$ate October and geese begin
to swim in squadrons
 tentatively airborne
they circle sketches of the lake
and land:
 tail-tipped
up on their white butts
their black necks like feathered snakes
while
three small ducks, almost too light for sailing,
bob like leaves.

Winter

"I Dig out the Velvety Moss, Earth Sweet."

In early winter,
Mother and I have a thing going.
Whoever sees the first snow,
no matter how light the fall,
tells the other.
This year, I saw it first—
small, round and loose—
turning into water
as it touched the ground.

Each Saturday afternoon,
my mother, my father and I
go to the Etruscan
museum. They are old, ancient
people these Etruscans.
I like the silence
at the museum.
I also like the small
statues, the sharp stone
hunting weapons
and the vases.
I try to find vases
that are whole,
but each has
at least one crack.

$\mathcal{E}$very Christmas
my father pays three musicians
to stop at our door
every morning
for one full week
and play novenas,
songs of Christ,
songs of peace.
One plays a flute,
one a drum, and one a
trombone. Some
mornings, they come to play
so early, they wake us up.
But we always open the door,
and, when they're finished,
thank them.
We always sing
the songs
they play.

$\mathcal{I}$ take the long walk
through cobblestone streets
and the little Jesus church
at the end of town,
past the valley
and the still wheel of the mill,
and slowly climb
the damp and slippery hill
that slopes
like the back of a giant.
On my hands and knees,
I dig out the velvety moss,
earth sweet.
The dirt and the December chill
hurt my hands,
but I carefully rip
chunks of the moist, green moss.
The silent shepherd,
serious Mary and Joseph,
and the open-armed baby
wait for their carpet.
I hurry home.

When I was a child in Sicily, my entire family took part in the making of the Nativity manger. I would go to a hill outside our little town to gather a moss carpet for the manger floor. The moss gathering made me feel close both to the Baby Jesus and to nature. The links with nature (the real moss) and with Jesus were important: the manger and the birth of Jesus became reality. It wasn't merely a manger scene. It was the real thing.

$\mathcal{W}$hy should I complain
of being alone?
A slim, lone sparrow
hops alertly along the shoreline
eating.

This Valentine's Day,
Mother and Father and I
went to the pet store
and bought ten lovebirds.
We took them home,
and then, from our
backyard, we let them fly.

EPILOGUE

Joy of an Immigrant, a Thanksgiving

*L*ike a bird grown weak in a land
where it always rains
and where all the trees have died,
I have flown long and long
to find sunlight pouring over branches
and leaves. I have journeyed, oh God,
to find a land where I can build a dry nest,
a land where my song can echo.

Letter from Sicily

We haven't eaten the grape
from the vineyard by the sea.
That creek where we used to wash
the grape is now dry;
the water loses itself
in the fields.
Return, dear friend,
for one more picnic
on a hill,
under the stars,
where we may dance.

INDEX OF FIRST LINES

ACKNOWLEDGMENTS

"After a long silence, / a few birds sing." first appeared in *Month-by-Month Poems*, Scholastic, Inc.

"Below the hill, the cemetery sits, / a small city of the perfectly behaved." first appeared in *Halloween Poems*, Holiday House.

"I pull a baby crab / off a seaweed-rich rock" first appeared in *Thanksgiving Poems*, Holiday House.

"In the early morning, / when Grandmother wakes" first appeared in *Poems for Grandmothers*, Holiday House.

"Late October and geese begin / to swim in squadrons" first appeared in *The New York Times*.

"My neighbor always buys a lamb / for Easter butchering" first appeared in *Easter Poems*, Holiday House.

"We haven't eaten the grape / from the vineyard by the sea" first appeared in *I Like You if You Like Me: Poems of Friendship*, Margaret McElderry Books.

The following poems first appeared in *Cricket* and *Spider* magazines:

"Each Saturday afternoon, / my mother, my father and I"—January 1999 *Cricket*

"Every Christmas / my father pays three musicians"—December 1999 *Cricket*

"I do cartwheels. / One day I'll cartwheel to a mountain,"—June 2002 *Spider*

"I like the feel of sand / between my toes."—May 1999 *Cricket*

"I like to watch / my mother dance."—May 1998 *Spider*

"I take the long walk / through cobblestone streets"—December 1988 *Cricket*

"In early winter, / Mother and I have a thing going."—December 2000 *Cricket*

"Like a bird grown weak in a land / where it always rains"—November 1987 *Cricket*

"Once, while eating bread, I bit my lip / and spilled a little blood:"—June 1996 *Cricket*

"The sun has a tail / that reaches under the earth"—April 1999 *Cricket*

"The wind from the northeast / is wild."—October 2001 *Cricket*

"This April night, / the moon is like a loose sunflower;"—April 1999 *Cricket*

"This Valentine's Day, / Mother and Father and I"—January 2001 *Cricket*

"Wingtips dancing, / stretching its shadow ahead of itself,"—May 1994 *Cricket*